11/16

FARM ANIMALS

ALPACAS

by Michelle Hasselius

Consultant: Anna Firshman, BVSc, PhD, DACVIM
Department of Veterinary Population Medicine
University of Minnesota

CAPSTONE PRESS
a capstone imprint

Pebble Plus is published by Capstone Press,
1710 Roe Crest Drive, North Mankato, Minnesota 56003.
www.mycapstone.com

Library of Congress Cataloging-in-Publication Data
Names: Hasselius, Michelle M., 1981– author.
Title: Alpacas / by Michelle Hasselius.
Other titles: Pebble plus. Farm animals.
Description: North Mankato, Minnesota : Capstone Press, [2017] | Series:
Pebble plus. Farm animals | Includes bibliographical references and index.
Identifiers: LCCN 2015051489| ISBN 9781515709244 (library binding) | ISBN 9781515709633 (pbk.)
| ISBN 9781515710981 (ebook (pdf))
Subjects: LCSH: Alpaca—Juvenile literature.
Classification: LCC SF401.A4 H37 2017 | DDC 636.2/966—dc23
LC record available at http://lccn.loc.gov/2015051489

Editorial Credits
Michelle Hasselius, editor; Kayla Rossow, designer; Pam Mitsakos, media researcher;
Katy LaVigne, production specialist

Photo Credits
Shutterstock: Aneta_Gu, 10–11, bluedogroom, 5, Dieter Hawlan, 6–7, Eky Studio, (back cover background),
Elenamiv, 22 (background), hjochen, 15, Karyl Miller, 13, Kookkai_nak, 1 (background), meunierd, 16–17, Milosz_G,
cover, 1, ostill, 19; Thinkstock: astonerattnet, 9, suefeldberg, 20–21

Note to Parents and Teachers

The Farm Animals series supports national science standards related to life science. This
book describes and illustrates alpacas. The images support early readers in understanding
the text. The repetition of words and phrases helps early readers learn new words. This
book also introduces early readers to subject-specific vocabulary words, which are defined
in the Glossary section. Early readers may need assistance to read some words and to use
the Table of Contents, Glossary, Read More, Internet Sites, and Index sections of the book.

Printed and bound in China.
007708

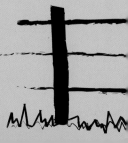

Table of Contents

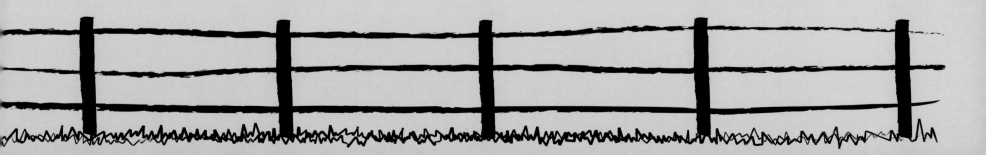

Meet the Alpacas

Alpacas wake up to

a new day on the farm.

They walk through the

field on padded feet.

They nibble on the grass.

Alpacas have soft hair called fleece or fiber. Alpaca fleece can be 22 different colors, including white, brown, black, and silver.

Farmers can own two different kinds of alpacas. Huacayas have short, wavy fleece. They look like teddy bears. Suri alpacas have silky, wavy fleece.

Huacaya (wuh-KAY-uh)
Suri (SUR-ee)

Suri alpacas

Alpacas are related to camels and llamas. But alpacas are smaller. They weigh up to 185 pounds (84 kilograms). Alpacas live about 20 years.

Adults and Babies

Alpacas grow up on the farm.

Baby alpacas are called crias.

Crias weigh about 17 pounds (7.7 kg)

at birth. Female alpacas are called

hembras. Males are called machos.

cria (KREE-uh)
hembra (em-BRAH)
macho (mah-CHOH)

crias

An alpaca eats grass and hay.
The chewed food travels into
one of the alpaca's three stomach
chambers. Later the alpaca burps
up the food and chews it again.

On the Farm

Alpacas stay together in a herd. They communicate by humming. Alpacas also make loud, high calls when scared or angry.

Farmers raise alpacas for their
fleece. Alpaca fleece is soft and
warm. Farmers shear the fleece
each spring. Fleece can be made
into clothing or blankets.

fleece

Foxes and other predators attack alpacas. Farmers use donkeys or dogs to keep predators away. Alpacas also need sheds. Alpacas stay safe on the farm.

Glossary

camel—an animal with a round hump on its back

chamber—an enclosed space in an animal's body

communicate—to share information, thoughts, or feelings

fleece—a coat of soft, fluffy hair that covers animals such as alpacas, sheep, and llamas; fleece is also called fiber

herd—a large group of animals that lives or moves together

hum—to make a steady, buzzing noise

nibble—to bite something gently

predator—an animal that hunts other animals for food

shear—to cut off or trim; a farmer shears an alpaca's fleece so it can be used to make cloth

shed—a small building

Read More

Cuddy, Robbin. *All About Drawing Farm & Forest Animals: Step-by-Step Illustrations.* Irvine, Calif.: Walter Foster, 2014.

Diaz, Joanne Ruelos. *Animals on the Farm.* Animals All Day! North Mankato, Minn.: Picture Window Books, 2014.

Dunn, Mary R. *Llamas.* South American Animals. Mankato, Minn.: Capstone Press, 2012.

Internet Sites

FactHound offers a safe, fun way to find Internet sites related to this book. All of the sites on FactHound have been researched by our staff.

Here's all you do:

Visit *www.facthound.com*

Type in this code: 9781515709244

 Check out projects, games and lots more at
www.capstonekids.com

Index